The Pain and Grief from *Losing* a Pet

Darrell Tolbert, Ph.D.

Dedication

I would like to dedicate this book to Mona, Patches, Spots, Nimbus, Zeus and Apollo who inspired me to write this book. I would also like to dedicate this book to all who have felt the pain from losing a beloved pet due to death. They left behind great memories that we will cherish forever! Grief has no time limit!

Contents

Acknowledgement

I would like to acknowledge my wife Kathy and my daughter Jireh for allowing me the time away from them to write this book. I would like to give great honor to the real VIP'S the Humane Society's across the world and the volunteers. Nothing but love and respect for all of you. A special shout out of Love to the No Kill Humane Society in my hometown Ocala Fl. You guys' Rock!

Preface

Death is a part of life but unfortunately it is a very painful experience. There are many of us who love our fur babies unconditionally. They are apart of our family. They have health and dental insurance. They have regular veterinarian visits and take heart worm prevention medication. I am Dr. Darrell Tolbert Pastor, Chaplain and the purpose for writing this book is to inform the reader about different painful experiences I have had throughout my lifetime as a result of a beloved pet.

I am an author of six other published books dealing with various topics. The inspiration for this book came from the death of my beloved female Boston Terrier Patches. She was my trucking buddy and as a result we shared many experiences and sceneries traveling over this beautiful country. Her death rocked my world and left me depressed for several months. Over a decade later a thought of her may bring a tear or two. As a result of the depression it inspired me to become a Pet Grief Counselor. Death can cripple a person holding them in that moment unable to move forward.

Stuck in yesterday thus robbing them of the Joy,Peace and Happiness of Today and Tomorrow! When it comes to children their feelings and emotions are often overlooked. However for many a death of a beloved pet is their first glimpsed of our enemy called death. It's the first painful tear in their little hearts. My job is to help heal and push forward those who within themselves are not able to. This book is to show my clients and readers that I speak from a point of experience that was learned through grief and pain. It is my deepest desire that those who read this book if they are struggling over the death of a beloved fur baby the stories will help them to heal and push forward.

Introduction

Death is a very painful experience that leaves our hearts broken into millions of pieces! Majority of the time, we focus on the loss of another human. However, there is a crowd that used to be overlooked until recently. That crowd includes all who have experienced the pain of losing a beloved pet.

Even though this book will mainly focus on my own pets, which were dogs and cats, it covers all pets. Horses, goats, cows, goldfish, turtles, snakes, monkeys, birds, squirrels, hamsters, pigs, lions, etc. It doesn't matter; the pain is all the same. When death takes away the pet we love dearly, it changes our lives. We were all created differently; some can lose a pet and bounce right back. Others may need help bouncing back into life.

I was created with the ability to feel others' pain and to have empathy and sympathy. Growing up, we had many dogs. I would always cry over the death of all our dogs. We had outside dogs, and all of them were males. Whenever a female dog in the neighborhood would go in heat, they would disappear for a day or two with a crowd of other male dogs chasing the one female. We had a German shepherd named Peewee. He would bite everyone who came into our yard. All the kids on the block hated him because of this. I think he had bitten just about all of them. He had gone missing for a day, then the next day, while all of us were playing in the yard, someone came and said, "I think your dog is dead besides the road on the main highway. A car hit him".

I believe I was around ten, eleven, or twelve years old at that time. I ran as fast as I could towards the highway, and from a distance, I could see a black dog beside the highway. Peewee was black, so that made me run even faster! I stopped when I came beside him, and the pain was unbelievable; it was Peewee. I picked his body up and threw him across my shoulders, and with tears coming out of my eyes, I walked home. Blood began to run from his nose all over my clothes, but I didn't care.

I kept walking and crying. As I approached home, some of the kids started laughing because they were glad, he was dead. Anger flashed through me, and I said, "every one of you who's laughing when I bury my dog, I am going to beat you up!" They became scared because they knew I could fight real good.

My mother came out of the house and saw me all bloody and in tears with the dog around my neck, and she said, "it's going to be alright stop crying and go bury him around the back of the house, then come take those bloody clothes off." I dug the hole and then buried him, but I didn't go immediately into the house. Now that I'm reliving it as I am writing this book, I think it's because his blood on me was a final connection to him, so I lingered around with those bloody clothes on. This is one of the main reasons why I became a Pet Bereavement Counselor. Oftentimes, the effects of the death of a pet on a kid are overlooked. As parents, our first response is to immediately replace that pet with another one.

Frequently we don't know what to say to our children, so we lie to them to spare them the pain of losing their pet. I told my nutritionist I was studying to become a Pet Bereavement Counselor, and she replied, "that's awesome. I could have used you a few weeks ago because our pet died. My three-year-old son came to me the next day and said mama, where is Buddy? I want to play with him. I told him that buddy was in heaven with Jesus. The following day he asked me when is Jesus going to send Buddy back so I could play with him? I told him that I didn't think Jesus is sending him back because he is having such a great time in doggie heaven."

She looked at me in the eyes and said I didn't know what to tell my poor son, so I told him that. The purpose of this book is to give tools that will help us deal with the death of a pet regardless of our age. If you are reading this book, it's a good guess that you have experienced the pain of losing a pet, so that puts us all into one big pet-loving family that can help each other get over this hurtful time in our lives. We are in a unique group because our pets are another family member to us. To those outside of our group, they may see them as just a dog, cat, etc. No, they are everything to us…Not just a dog!

Not "*Just a dog.*"

From time-to-time people told me to "Lighten up. It's just a dog, or that's a lot of money for just a dog."
They don't understand the distance traveled, the time spent, or the costs involved for "Just a dog."
Some of my proudest moments have come with "Just a dog."
Many hours have passed with my only company being "Just a dog," and not once have I felt slighted.
"Just a dog" brought some of my saddest moments.
In those days of darkness, the gentle touch of "Just a dog" was the only thing that gave me comfort and a purpose to overcome the day.
If you, too, think it's "Just a dog," you probably have no understanding of the phrases like "Just a friend," "Just a sunrise," or Just a promise."
"Just a dog" brought the essence of friendship, trust, and pure unbridled joy into my life
"Just a dog" brings out the compassion and patience that made me a better person.
Because of "Just a dog," I start imagining the rise early, taking long walks, and looking longingly into the future.
For folks like me, it's not "Just a dog." It embodies all the hopes and dreams of the future, the fond memories of the past, and the pure joy of the moment.
"Just a dog" brings out the good inside me and diverts my bad thoughts and all worries of my day.
I hope that someday people can understand it's not "Just a dog."
It's the thing that gives me humanity and keeps me from being "Just a man" or "just a woman."
So, the next time you hear the phrase "Just a dog," Smile because they "Just don't understand."

Author ~ Richard Biby

1
Mona

I owned a semi-truck business, and I worked locally during the time of this story. Once I came back from my route, I called my wife, and she said she was at her mother's house. When I arrived, I knocked on the door, and after I stepped inside, this Boston Terrier immediately went crazy. She was growling with her teeth showing and was very aggressive. My wife and sister-in-law were trying to calm her down. Where did this dog come from? I asked because I had never seen her before. My sister-in-law replied that she had found her walking through her neighborhood; she thought she had run away from her owner due to the fireworks. I looked at her real, close, gorgeous dog, but I didn't particularly care for small dogs back then. I felt they were a waste of dog food because they didn't instill fear in people, so they were not good guard dogs. This mindset came from my childhood because our dogs were mostly German Shepherds and bit people who would come into our yard. We also had a Pit-bull named Trouble, but he never bit anyone; however, he instilled fear in them just because of his breed.

Whenever another male walked into the house, Mona reacted the same way. We concluded that her owner was probably a man, and he was mistreating her because she didn't respond to females the way she responded to the presence of a man. Looking at this Boston Terrier, I had a very strong premonition she would end up in the apartment with us. Therefore, it made me speak out and ask bluntly, what will you do with her? The response was they would try to find her owner, and if they couldn't, they would take her to an animal shelter and see if she was microchipped. I looked at my wife and said, "I know you, so don't try to keep this dog.

Kathy was pregnant during this time and stayed with her mother for a few days during the week because she was on bed rest for the remainder of her pregnancy. After my visit, I left her at her mother's home, went to our apartment, and went to sleep. I woke up around 5 am and went to work. I had a great day. I called Kathy, and she informed me she was at the apartment. When I opened the door to the apartment, I was greeted by Mona's aggressive growling and white teeth gnarling at me. I immediately became angry and shouted, "what is this dog doing here? I told you not to try and keep this dog. She replied Linda wanted to keep her, but her husband didn't want an inside dog.

I responded I don't blame him! I don't want her inside either. When I was a kid, all our dogs lived outside and only came inside on freezing nights, or sometimes, they would follow behind someone as they went in and out of the house. She replied I would take her to the shelter and see if she is chipped. "Kathy, we are not going to keep this dog, I said. Her reply was alright, I heard you the first time." The suspicion returned, the feeling that this dog would become a part of our family regardless of whether I liked it or not. Kathy kept her in our bathroom. The next morning when I went to the bathroom to brush my teeth and get ready for work, I was met with the same aggression. I thought to myself, "you will be gone by the time I return from work.

When I returned home, I was again greeted with the same aggression because guess who was still there? You guessed it, Ms. Mona. Lol. "Kathy, why is this dog still here???" In her whiney high-pitched voice, Kathy responded, "I took her to the shelter, but she doesn't have a chip, so I brought her back home. I couldn't just leave her there." I was upset over this because I didn't want another dog. Yes, I had them growing up as a kid, but I was now around thirty-seven. The last dog I owned was around the age of eighteen. After I left for the military, I never desired to have another dog, especially a small dog, as I stated before I felt they were a waste of dog food. Then to make matters worse, when I went into my office, I saw Mona had decided to wage war against me by using my office as a bathroom.

I began shouting when I saw this big pile of dog mess on the carpet in my office. This dog must go! Mona knew this was my office, and this was her way of getting even with me for not wanting her to stay here with us! Kathy came and cleaned up the big pile of mess and said maybe if you stop talking mean to her, she won't poop in your office. Why can't we keep her? I walked outside so I could settle down. I thought about my wife and how she had miscarried our baby about six months before this pregnancy. I knew she was still hurt by it; therefore, I concluded that Mona would offer companionship while I was at work and help aid in her emotional healing.

I went inside and said you can keep her, but I am not responsible. She is one hundred percent your responsibility. I am not paying for food, vet bills, nothing…absolutely nothing. She was so happy and excited. The next morning, I went into the bathroom, and Mona greeted me with the growling as usual. I looked her in the eyes and said, "Since you are going to stay here, we need to get along, therefore you need to stop all of your growling." I reached out and touched her on her head. She allowed me to touch her, but the snarling was still there just a little lower-key than usual. The third morning I entered the bathroom, I was shocked, no growling. She was happy to see me, but little did she know I had a treat in my pocket. I had a piece of meat that I rewarded her with.

We were becoming the best of friends. When I came home from work, she greeted me at the door instead of running into the bathroom. I was walking her one day, and she changed my belief in small dogs. A big dog ran out towards me, and I was glad she was on a leash because she ran towards him, growling and barking and ready to fight to protect me from this dog. I was proud of her and was now madly in love with the Boston Terrier breed. Mona was a beautiful black and white Boston. Her coat was shiny, and she had a Haggerty dot or Spot. I didn't know anything about a Haggerty spot, but later, I learned only a few Boston's had it. That particular marking can trace its origins back to the Haggerty family of the early 1900s. The Haggerty family was a well-known and respected Boston breeder of their time.

One morning, I left out of the front door to go to work, and as I was walking to my car, I realized that I had left something. When I opened the door, Mona was looking out of my bedroom door at me. I found that very odd. It was like she was waiting for me to leave for some reason, and because I came back in, I had caught her by surprise. Later that night, when I was talking to Kathy, Mona suddenly jumped into bed with us and looked away. I said to Kathy there is no way you can tell me this is the first time this dog has jumped into this bed. I always had a love for dogs but not enough love to allow them in my bed. She replied one morning after you left, she came out of the bathroom and jumped into bed with me, so I let her stay.

Every morning since then, she waits for you to leave, then she comes and jumps into bed with me. Then it hit me; that's why she was looking at me this morning. She was in the room with you when I left, but when she heard me coming back in, she came back out to see who was coming into the house. I looked at Mona and said, "you are a smart dog. You are the first dog I have allowed to be in my bed." Mona loved me, but she was devoted to Kathy. We learned that the first person a Boston loves is the person who has their loyalty.

She loved Kathy first, so she was devoted to her for that reason. Mona had stolen my heart; I was the one who had taken over the responsibility of feeding her every morning. After that, we became the best of friends. One day, I was walking her, and a German Shepherd came running from a house in our neighborhood towards us. Mona immediately went into a protective mood. Her hair stood on her back, and she tried to run toward the dog, but I had her on a leash, so I pulled her back. I was proud of her; this was the second moment that helped to solidify my thoughts about small dogs. They are aggressive and will protect their owner. One day, Kathy decided to stay with her mother, so she took Mona with her. I was at a store in Orlando, FL unloading my truck at a grocery store when I received a phone call from Kathy screaming and hollering. I couldn't understand her words because she was distressed about something. I immediately panicked because she had miscarried in the past; I thought she had miscarried again. I shouted "what's wrong? I couldn't understand her because she was screaming and crying hysterically. I yelled calm down so I can understand you. She said Mona had been hit by a car! Immediately Pain shot through my body. How did it happen? Is she dead? She replied she left out of mama's yard and went across the road to use the bathroom, and when I came to the door, she got excited about seeing me and came flying back across the road while a car was coming. The car hit her and made her flip over, but she jumped up, ran to my feet, and laid down. .

I yelled take her to the vet now! I don't care how much it costs! Take her now! She replied okay. When she hung up, I stood outside my semi-truck and began praying to God. I said God, you have all power in your hands. Please save my dog. Please don't let her die! I went back into the store and continued to take the products off with my pallet jack; however, my mind was in turmoil. Kathy called back about an hour later, screaming again. She said they put a tube down her throat, and it filled up with blood. She is bleeding from the inside, and they suggested I put her to sleep.

Pain beyond belief shot through my body! Tears began to flow! I cried for Mona, I cried for myself, and I cried for my wife. I knew how much she loved Mona. I told her I was almost finished; I would be home immediately and try not to stress too much or get too excited because of the baby. When I got off the phone, anger toward God began. I was a licensed ordained Minister, and I was doing street ministry. The streets were filled with crack addicts roaming back and forth through the street's night and day during this time; my ministry set up speakers in these high-crime areas. I would feed the drug addicts BBQ chicken and other side dishes; not only did the ministry feed those on drugs, but also the prostitutes, alcoholics, and drug dealers.

Before we gave them the food, I would preach a message and then pray for their deliverance from their addiction. About a decade before I started my street ministry, I used to sell crack cocaine to many of those same people I was preaching, praying, and crying with. After getting out of the military in February 1999, I became influenced by the money the drug dealers were making. I eventually became one myself; however, I had an encounter with God that changed my life. Once I was a part of the problem in the community, but because of a relationship with God, I was now a part of the solution in the community.

My Semi trucking business paid for all the food; I felt obligated to give back to the community I took from. I had been faithful to this calling by God. Now I found myself angry at Him! I said I didn't ask you for a lot of money! I didn't ask you for a big house or an expensive car! I asked for something very simple for you to do. I go into those streets, putting my life in danger to reach people for You. Many may have aids or other diseases, but I still hugged them and prayed with them. They cry all over my shirt, many have an unpleasant body odor from a lack of bathing, but I still hugged them with genuine love and compassion. The least you could do because of all I do in the community for You is to grant a very simple request from me, your servant, to save my dog.

I was so mad until I thought about never doing another street service again. He let my Mona die! That resentment towards God lasted for a while. I was hurt over the death of my dog, and at that time, it seemed to me that God didn't even care! When I arrived, the vet sent her body home in a box. I opened it to take one last look at Mona. With tears in my eyes, I buried her on the side of my mother-in-law's house because we lived in an apartment. I knew we would move one day, so I wanted her body in a place I could always visit. Of course, I did the one thing I learned from taking the course to become a bereavement counselor, which you should never do, which was to immediately begin to find a replacement for my beloved pet Mona.

2
Patches

Some think a replacement will help the healing process go faster, and I was one of those people. I felt my wife needed another companion to be there with her during her pregnancy. Therefore, about a month later, she put an ad up for a Boston Terrier for $300. I didn't know how expensive Boston Terriers puppies were. They sell anywhere from $800 to $1500 and more. To our surprise, someone with a Boston responded to the ad a few days later. We were excited and set up a meeting place at a Winne Dixie store in our city. As we were waiting, a person in a station wagon with two people in it and two dogs pulled up to us. I asked, "Are you the people with Boston?" and they replied, "yes."

They got out, opened the back door, pulled out this small female Boston, and walked her over to me. I was deeply disappointed! Mona was gorgeous. Her coat had a shine; she had a Haggerty dot on her head, but this Boston was the total opposite. Something was wrong with one of her eyes. When I asked the lady about it, she said a wasp had stung her in the eye. God is my witness; I had never seen so many fleas on one dog in my whole life. They were running and jumping all over her. There were so many fleas my wife said the areas of fleas looked like areas of black hair. I looked at the people and wondered how they could allow a dog to have so many fleas on her. They had two other bigger dogs in the car, so I knew they were probably covered with fleas also. Then I looked at the man and woman and formed my opinion of them. Trust me, my opinion was not a very godly opinion!

I looked at Kathy and said no, I didn't want her, but when I looked down at the dog again, she was looking up at me, and as our eyes locked on each other, sorrow filled my heart. It was if she was saying sir please save me from this horrible situation! I knew I had to save her from these cruel people. I said I will give you one hundred dollars for her. They immediately responded we would take it. I gave them the money, and they went on their way. I told Kathy to hold her by the leash while I went into the store to purchase some flea killer. When I returned, Kathy said this dog walks with a limp, which I had not noticed previously. Now I had someone who walked like me. Since I had pain in my left hip, I walked with a limp also.

I applied the gel to her back, and the fleas went crazy, jumping everywhere. We waited about thirty minutes, giving them time to die or jump off. I then jumped into a dumpster behind the store to get a box to put her in. She still had fleas on her, so I put her in the box and closed the lid, so they won't jump into my car. Once home, I bathed her outside, getting most of the fleas off, but she kept getting muddy in the dirt, so I took her into the house and put her in the tub. As I was bathing her, I fell in love with Patches, she wasn't a Mona, but she was beautiful in her own way. I now had a trucking buddy to ride with me across the United States.

Patches and I had a show on Facebook called Patches and the Preacher man. I pretended Patches could talk, and we had different conversations. Many people loved it and would comment on the post. Many would say hello to Patches. Patches also knew how to rap; her rap name was MC Patchalo. One of my most memorable moments with her was this. We both loved smoked turkey legs; we would stop at this Petro Truck Stop that sold them in Orange Lake, FL. I would pull enough meat off the leg to fill her bowl and then eat the rest. I would always stop at the fuel pumps, then go inside and purchase the turkey leg. This one particular time when I returned to the truck, I unwrapped it and took a bite.

I left it on the dashboard and jumped out to pump my fuel; Patches jumped in the seat and looked out the window at me, then she disappeared back into the truck. A few minutes later, she looked out the window at me again and disappeared. A few minutes again, she looked out at me and then disappeared back into the truck. I thought to myself, Patches is acting strangely, let me go and see what she is doing. I climbed back into the truck and Patches was enjoying our turkey leg without me. Lol.

I learned unconditional love through her. I recall once Patches had to use the bathroom. It was cold, and there was snow on the ground. The temperature was around thirty degrees. I put her on the ground to use the bathroom, and she wouldn't do anything. After several attempts, it dawned on me, a Florida boy, there was no grass for her to pee or poop on. I had to clear away the snow for her. I would have to pick her up in the cold and dig through the snow until I found grass; then, I had to clear out a spot large enough to put her down in.

She always had to take her time; many times, I would have to say please, Patches, use the bathroom. It's freezing out here. One time I took the batteries cables off; to clean the batteries however, when I put them back on, I out of ignorance left off the wire that controlled the computer, which controlled the heat. We had a run from Florida to Minnesota. It was wintertime, and I noticed Patches in the back bed shaking by the time we made it to Chicago. I pulled over and said "what's wrong girl? The heat isn't working back here. I turned the bunk heater on, and nothing but cold air. I wrapped her in the quilt on the bed and started driving again until we reached our destination in Minnesota. It was around twenty degrees, and we had no heat.

I plugged in a heating pad and put it under the sheet on the bed, I grabbed patches and pulled the heavy quilt over us, and it was so warm under there. The next morning the truck was so cold inside when I pulled the cover off my head, I noticed that the water in Patches' water bowl was frozen solid! I left Patches under the quilt and got dressed in the cold. I called my job and informed them that I had no heat and would have to find a freight liner dealership if it didn't warm up. We were unloaded and went to an off-brand truck stop to wait for the reload to take us back to FL. Another driver from the same company was waiting for his reload. I knew him and told him about the heat problem in the truck. By this time, nothing was working because of the computer, so the heating pad no longer worked because the sockets it plugged into were now dead.

I went into the truck stop and saw they had a trucker lounge. However, no pets were allowed inside. There was no way I was going to be inside in the heat and leave Patches outside freezing in the truck. I devised a plan; I had a big winter jacket that went below my knee. It was big enough to hide Patches under it, and I went into the lounge and sat in a recliner chair. I reclined in the chair, which caused Patches to lay comfortably on my chest. The other driver came in and said they called me with a reload, but I told them to give it to you because you don't have any heat. I thanked him, then they called me with the reload instructions.

Once I arrived at the reload about twenty minutes later, the other driver arrived. He said they had two loads here. We were loaded simultaneously; he said since you don't have any heat, put Patches in my truck and allow her to ride in the heat with me. I was grateful to him for this; we pulled over when we made it to the southern part of Illinois because he was going a different way. I thanked him, put Patches back in my truck, wrapped her back in the quilt, and headed south toward the heat. When I made it to Lake City, FL, I went to the Freightliner dealership and found out I had left the chord off when I connected the battery cables back on. Of course, I was upset because our freezing resulted from my ignorance. However, it was a bonding experience for Patches and me.

After a few years, Patches decided she wanted to retire from trucking. Kathy took us to the truck, however Patches refused to get out of the car. When I would come to the driver's side to get her, she would run to the passenger's side. She would run to the driver's side when I walked around to the passenger side. This was strange behavior because she loved trucking. We concluded her behavior resulted from us getting another dog, and she wanted to stay behind to watch over our daughter, who was now three years old. I allowed her to stay, putting an end to Patches and the Preacher man over the roadshow.

We had health insurance on all our pets, and at one of her check-ups, it was discovered that she had high blood pressure. I was shocked to discover that dogs could develop several human diseases. She was given medication to take for her high blood pressure. I concluded it probably resulted from our bad eating habits over the years. Hot dogs,

Cheeseburgers, and only God knows what else.

When I came home one day, I noticed her stomach looked swollen, and when I squeezed it, it was hard. She was acting normally with her happy-go-lucky self. Jumping up and down on me and being her usual playful self. The next day, as I was leaving, I told my wife to keep an eye on her stomach and if it didn't go down, take her to the vet. I returned home two days later, and she was still her chipper self, but her stomach didn't seem like it had improved. Kathy said she was acting odd while I was gone. She told me Patches went into the bathroom and pulled some of my clothes out of the dirty clothes basket, and she had been sleeping on them. Instantly, I knew something was seriously wrong. I arrived home at night; I said take her to the vet in the morning because something wasn't right. That night she would not go to sleep, so I put her in bed to comfort her. I said, "what's wrong, girl? Lay down. I am home. It's okay to relax." I kissed her on the head, and sometime during the night, she fell asleep. I kissed her on her head, not knowing that would be the last kiss I would ever give her. Unknown to me, that kiss was a goodbye kiss.

I was in Kentucky when I received my life's most painful phone call. Kathy was crying with ear-piercing screams. She said I took her to the vet as you told me, and when they stuck this tube into her belly, it was full of blood. Her pulmonary heart valve has been ripped, and its leaking blood inside of her stomach. Her doctor said the surgery would be super expensive, and her pet insurance doesn't cover it, and he suggests you give the okay for her to be put to sleep. That news sent penetrating pain through my body like lightning striking a tree. This same illness had happened to my cousin, who also had high blood pressure and because he wasn't taking his blood pressure medication properly. Even though my wife used the words put her to sleep, I heard, permit THEM TO KILL MY PATCHES! I began to panic, and the tears were flowing. I asked, "how much is the surgery?" She replied, "around $7000." I replied, "ask the doctor if I paid the $7000 for the surgery can he guarantee me she would live."

My Patches was worth more than seven thousand dollars to me! If he said yes, I would write a check so fast that heads would spin. Kathy asked him, and he said he couldn't guarantee me the surgery would be successful because she was old, and even putting her under anesthesia was risky. At that moment, I was stuck with the hardest decision I ever made in my adult life. About ten years later, my siblings and I made the decision to disconnect my father from the ventilator. I watched him take his last breath. That hurt so much, and of course, I loved my father dearly, but the pain that came with this decision was incomparable. I said, "I will be back in two days. I want to see Patches before I make that decision. Take her home!" She replied the doctor said that is not a good decision because she is in pain, and it would be unfair to leave her in this condition for two days until you returned home." I replied go get Jireh (my daughter, who was almost four at this time) and allow her to say her goodbyes to Patches. Then, you can put her to sleep.

I called my mother very panic-stricken. She screamed, "what's wrong? I said I had to put Patches to sleep because she was bleeding from her heart. She screamed pull that truck over right now before you kill yourself because you are in no condition to drive. Everyone knew how much I loved Patches. I kept crying as I pulled over into a rest area and crawled into my bed. The pain was so deep, and the tears would not stop gushing from my eyes. I kept saying Patches Daddy is sorry for putting you to sleep, but there was no other way! I love you more than words can describe! My son called and said, "Daddy, are you alright? I heard about Patches, and I know how much you loved that dog. You loved that dog more than you loved me. I remember you said if it came between Patches and me having to leave the house, I better pack my bags because Patches wasn't going anywhere."

I told Kathy to bring her body home and put her into the extra deep freezer we had in the garage, and I would bury her myself when I returned home two days later. When I arrived home, I removed the frozen body from the deep freezer and took one last look at her. With tears coming out of my eyes we buried her at my mother-in-law's home next to Mona. As I stated earlier, I knew I would be purchasing my own home soon, and I wanted her body in a place where I could visit whenever I wanted. I went into a depression over her death, and even today, twelve years later, I still cry over thoughts of her. While I was writing this part of the book about her death, I cried. There is no specific time for us to heal when it comes to the death of our beloved pets. Patches, my beloved daughter...

A million words would not bring you back!
Daddy knows because he tried!
Neither would a million tears!
Daddy knows because he cried!
Putting you down was the hardest decision,
Daddy had to make!
If there is a heaven for pets, I pray
You made it
Through those pearly gates.
You taught me unconditional love and protected me from all harm and danger until the end!
Your death broke daddy's heart into a million pieces
And I pray that in the next life, we are united again!

3

Spotsy & Nimbus and Zeus & Apollo

believe Spotsy coming into the house and becoming a part of the family was the main reason Patches stopped riding in the truck. There was a new dog in the house, and maybe she needed to stay home and keep an eye on her. Spotsy was a tiny dog. She was a three lb. fully grown Chihuahua. My sister-in-law had a neighbor who could no longer care for her due to a cancer diagnosis. She was well taken care of. Unlike Patches, she came with polished paw nails, nice matching collar, and no fleas. At first, I didn't want her. I always gave the same rules to my wife and my daughter. This pet is your responsibility; I am not buying food or cleaning cages. Once the pet is settled in and becomes a part of our family, I always end up paying for all the food and cleaning out cages. This happened with her hamster (Boxer) and guinea pig (Butterscotch), but she was my baby girl. Therefore, she was spoiled and Daddy's little girl, so I normally ended up giving in to her wishes.

After Patches died, Spotsy was the only pet in the house, and I saw firsthand that pets grieved over the death of another pet they lived with and formed a family bond. Spotsy refused to eat for about three days or more after Patches death. Finally, she slowly started to eat again, and that's when Nimbus the cat came into the house. A dear family friend, our daughter's godmother, had cats, and one day, I came home, and there was Nimbus and his cat litter box. I initially rejected it but gave in with the same instructions: I would not buy food or clean the cat litter box. This lasted about one month, and after that month was over,

I found myself cleaning out the litter box, which caused me to bond with him. When we first acquired Nimbus, we thought he was a girl and therefore my daughter named him Nimzey. Two months later, we made an appointment at the vet to have her spay and found out she was a He. His testicles had not dropped and that was the cause of confusion.

Upon one of Spots' (Spotsy) scheduled check-ups at the Veterinarian, it was discovered that she had a small hole in her skull resulting from a congenital disability where her skull didn't form completely. This left a soft spot on the top of her small head, the same as the soft Spot in an infant's head. Fortunately for her, this congenital disability would save her life in a future accident. One Saturday, my wife and I were sleeping in bed, and we heard Jireh screaming. I jumped up as the bedroom door opened, and she held Spot's limp body. I screamed, "what happened to her? Between sobs, she said I was throwing her up and catching her, but I missed this time, and her head hit the floor, and I think she is dead. I grabbed Spots from her and, out of fear, started yelling at my daughter and telling her Spots was badly injured. I apologized later because she was only four years old at the time. My wife drove while we rushed to her vet.

Her eyes were cloudy, and her tongue was hanging out of her mouth. I said, it's okay, Baby Girl; we are taking you to the vet. I put my hand over her head and began to pray to God. Please let her be okay for my daughter's sake because she won't forgive herself if Spots dies. Once at the vet, they said they were not equipped to handle a head injury like this and recommended a more advanced Veterinarian clinic. We rushed over to the clinic and checked her in. We had to pay $600 before they did any treatment or X-rays. I paid for it, and the X-rays showed there was damage, and her brain was swelling; they didn't know if she would live. They said they had to keep her so they could monitor her during the night; if she made it through the night, she might recover.

We went home. All of us were very sad. Jireh asked how Spots is doing and would she be okay? I said she will be okay, Baby. She said Daddy, I didn't mean to hurt Spots.

I replied, "I know, and I am sorry for yelling at you. We will check on her in the morning. That night I sent so many prayers up to heaven for her healing.

When we returned the next morning, we received great news that the swelling was going down. The hole in her skull saved her. If her skull had been completely closed, the pressure from her brain swelling might have killed her. However, since there was a hole in her skull, the pressure was released through it. We were allowed to take her home, but she had to learn to stand and walk again. I will never forget this moment. She couldn't walk the first day we brought her home. The next day when I came home from work, they had her on the sofa, lying in her bed.

I sat on the other end down from her. Immediately she came out of her bed, trying to walk toward me. She fell but got back up and stumbled towards me until she reached me and climbed into my lap. We shouted in joy over her progress. Kathy started crying because this was a sign that she would be okay. However, now I knew she loved me the most because she didn't attempt to walk toward anyone except me, lol. It took her about three weeks to recover and fully return to her normal self. About two years later, I purchased my own home. I never lost the desire for another Boston Terrier. I had promised my daughter I would get her one. We put out a post on Facebook and a lady responded. I arranged a meeting to see her puppy.

The lady stated that she didn't like dogs, but her sister had two, and she thought if she sent him to her anyway, she would fall in love with him. She never bonded with him. I drove an hour and a half to meet her. She pulled into the parking lot where I was eagerly waiting, and a beautiful red Boston puppy got out. I was in love immediately!!! His collar had his name on the tag. It read Oliver. I gave her the money, and she gave him to me with his cage and toys. He was only five or six months old and had a Haggerty Spot. Oliver was Haggerty! I looked at his paws and noticed how big they were, so I knew he wouldn't be an average-sized Boston. At that moment, I didn't realize just how right I was. I decided his name wasn't fitting for the awesome dog he would become, so Kathy suggested the name Zeus! When we walked into the house, Nimbus ran and climbed to the top of his cat pole. Spots sat up in her bed. All eyes were on this new visitor in the home.

Zeus walked up to Spots, and they touched noses, then Spots backed away. Nimbus had this look of disapproval over another member added to the family. He figured that two were company, but three was a crowd. I laid back on the sofa to get a quick nap. Once I dosed off, I was awakened by a loud whimpering from pain. I jumped up to discover Nimbus had come down and attacked Zeus. I think Spots had told Nimbus to let the new guy know how things are run around here. Tell him I called the shots even though I am the smallest and you are my enforcer. From that day forward, Zeus knew Spot Lil three lb. behind called the shots and Nimbus was the enforcer. Soon they would grow in love with each other. Spots was getting up in age; after each vet check-up, she was always given a negative report.

She started having digestive problems and had to be put on this expensive dog food promoting intestinal health. You couldn't purchase it without a prescription from the doctor. Her food cost one hundred dollars a month, but I didn't mind paying it because we loved Spots. I noticed she had started sleeping a lot, and I feared that the end of this life was getting closer. She was Jireh's pet, and she loved her so much, therefore I knew Spot's death would devastate her! Her legs started bothering her, so she couldn't go on walks like she used to. One day I passed a yard sale and saw a baby stroller for sale. I purchased it so I could put Spots in it while we walked Zeus. Every morning, I would check on her to ensure she was still alive.

One day, I came home, and asked Kathy where Spots is. She replied she is in bed resting but was up earlier using the bathroom. A few hours passed, and I asked Kathy if the pets had eaten dinner. She said Zeus ate, but Spots has been sleeping most of the day since breakfast, but I will wake her up to feed her. While sitting in my office, I hear Kathy calling Spots' name to wake her up. Then I heard her screaming oh my God, Spots is dead! I jumped up in unbelief because I knew she had slept in a deep sleep one time before, and we thought she had died, but she was just in a deep sleep. I rushed to her bed, and pain ripped through my heart because she was cold and stiff when I grabbed her. I picked her body up and cried. I cried from the pain I was feeling, and the pain I knew would snatch my daughter's heart out.

Jireh had left with her grandmother, I told Kathy to call her mother and tell her to bring Jireh home but don't let her know Spots had died. While I was in the front of my house crying and digging a hole to bury her, my mother-in-law's car pulled into the driveway, and Jireh got out.

She walked toward me and asked Daddy what's wrong? Why are you crying? I said Spots have passed away! She ran into the house, and I heard a scream I will never forget!!! It was overflowing and gripped with pain! Pain from the soul! I have been to many funerals, but I have never heard a scream like that before. I rushed into the house, and she had Spots' body in her arms, rocking back and forth on the floor, screaming to the top of her voice. Her grandmother was trying to stop her from crying, but I said to let her cry and hold her as long as she wanted because Spots was her dog; she was her baby.

After about fifteen or twenty minutes, she put her body down so gently. She entered her room, came out with some of Spots' clothes, and dressed her into them. Then she wrapped her into a blanket and said, "Daddy, now you can bury her. I put a box in front of her, and she gently placed Spots into it. I sealed the top, and we went out and buried her in the flower garden on our front lawn. Zeus and Nimbus weren't themselves for a few days. I could tell they were missing Spots. Nimbus walked all through the house, including the bedrooms looking for her.

Every morning Nimbus greeted me at the bathroom door. I would close the door and see a paw come under the door while sitting on the toilet. I would touch his paw, and he would jerk it back out, then push it back under the door, and when I touched it again, he would jerk it back out.

We played that game every morning. Nimbus was a smart cat with a great personality with plenty of life to live. He was only two, but he was a big powerful cat and highly intelligent. We had developed our morning routine. I played our game in the bathroom, cleaned out his cat litter box, and then I would fix his breakfast. I noticed that he wasn't meeting at the bathroom door some mornings, and his cat litter box was still clean from the day before. Kathy told me he had vomited up his food a few times. I had a vet appointment scheduled for him out of concern for his health. Kathy and Jireh took him, and God knows I didn't expect the phone call I received. Kathy was crying and said the vet said he was in stage four kidney failure, and he was confused because a cat that was young and in great shape like Nimbus never had kidney problems.

He said that somehow, he had gotten poison into his system that damaged his kidneys. He was an inside cat. He feared the outside, so we didn't know where the poison would come from. The vet said he was suffering; therefore, we should put him down. When you send your cat to the vet thinking you will get a simple report of some stomach virus, and you get a death report. That pain you know so very well from the other three pets hits you again. The tears flow as you give the okay, knowing that only three months ago, my daughter was devastated over the loss of her beloved Spots' death. Now she must experience the death of her cat. In less than three months, Spots and Nimbus were gone leaving only Zeus. I dug another hole on the side of the house. They had taken Zeus with them, and Kathy sent me a picture of Zeus with his head lying on the box that contained his brother Nimbus' body.

Poor Zeus was in pain and grieving! We tearfully buried Nimbus, but the pain from the two close deaths lingered. Zeus stopped eating for a few days and slept a lot. When he was awake, there was no life in him. He was grieving badly. I decided he needed companionship to help him, and my daughter overcome their pain. As I stated before getting another pet doesn't always make the grief process go away. We need to talk about our feelings and allow the grief process to take its course. I decided instead of buying a new Boston puppy, I would rescue one from the Humane Society. I received an alert from a Human Society concerning a mixed Boston Terrier dog.

I went to see him, and even though he wasn't a full-blooded Boston, I decided to rescue him. I sent a video to my wife, and she liked him. His name was Olaf. I paid the adoption fee and brought him home to surprise my daughter. She loved him, but we changed his name to Apollo to match Zeus. Apollo came with luggage! He played all day, tore up socks, chewed on furniture, dog beds, etc. He was playful all the time. Full speed ahead without stopping. Kathy took him to the vet for his first check-up, and he was going crazy trying to get to another dog in the vet's office. He is super aggressive toward anyone who even looks at us and especially toward other dogs. The doctor said I had seen about twenty dogs like him. He has mental problems; (I am not making this stuff up). The vet said his brain doesn't shut off. I bet he plays all day long, doesn't he? She replied yes. He said Apollo would have to undergo expensive behavior training, which might not help him. Obedience training will not help a dog like this. Only mental therapy and behavior training might give him a chance to be normal like other dogs.

He gave Kathy a prescription for Prozac to help keep him calm and a script for Xanax. About two months later after bringing him home from the Humane Society his behavior had not improved, therefore Kathy said we take him back to the shelter. I said we will not take him back. He needs to be loved. One time Kathy gave him a Prozac pill. He walked over to me, jumped up on my legs, and looked into my eyes. I could see those drugs had him in a daze. I told Kathy never give him one of those pills again. I started training him and showing him love. He stopped chasing other dogs. He whined when a dog would pass by the house, but he sat there obediently. He keeps Zeus in tip-top shape by playing with him all day. I thank God for Apollo. He is a great benefit to our family. He gives so much love to us; it's like he is so grateful for being rescued from the Humane Society.

Patches Pet Pain and Grief Counseling Services established the Apollo Fund on behalf of Apollo to give at least ten percent of its profit to the no-kill shelter to help with the expenses it takes to keep the animals with food and medical care. If you are struggling with losing a pet, please seek help because we are trained in these areas.

- People and Animals.
- The Stages of Grief.
- How Your Clients Feel.
- Immediate Help.
- Healing with Therapy.
- Therapy Tools.
- Grief Disorders

I send my condolences, love, and sympathy to all who have experienced or are still experiencing the pain and grief of losing a pet. You can contact me at 352-361-8473 or 786-897-4744. Email Ljireh@ aol.com; if you live in another state or city, I also do counseling through zoom. This book exposes you to the pain I have experienced; therefore, I believe my scars are to heal others in this area.

About the Author

[Dr. Darrell Tolbert is a licensed Chaplain and the Pastor of L-Jireh Ministries in Ocala Fl. He is the author of seven published books which can be found on Amazon and many other outlets. He is the owner of Cushite Financial Services, V-1 Rotate! Motivate! Motivational business. Website https://www.rotateelevate.com

His education includes graduate of United Bible College, Enrolled into American Bible Academy, Master degree in Divinity, Honorary Doctorate Degree in Theology, Doctorate Degree in Divinity and a Ph.D. Philosophy in Christian Living. He is the owner and professor at the Open Bible College extension in Ocala Fl. He is married to Kathy Tolbert, and they have five children. Nathan, Durrell, Darreka, Jaleica and L-Jireh Tolbert.